How to Start a Van and Box Truck Business

Understanding the Van and Box Truck Business Landscape

Ella Nelson

Table of Contents

INTRODUCTION

Ever dreamed of ditching the cubicle and becoming your own boss? Picture this: cruising down the open highway, the sun glinting off your freshly waxed van, the radio blasting your favorite tunes, and the freedom to call your own shots. Sounds pretty good, right? Well, that could be your reality in the exciting world of van and truck businesses.

This book is your roadmap to turning that dream into a thriving reality. Whether you're a handyman with a knack for repairs, a budding entrepreneur with big ideas, or simply someone tired of the corporate grind, starting a van and truck business can be the ticket to a fulfilling and profitable career.

But don't let the open road fool you. There are potholes and detours along the way. This book is your GPS, guiding you through every step of the journey, from choosing the right vehicle and service offerings to finding customers and growing your business. We'll cover:

Picking Your Lane: Exploring the diverse world of van and truck businesses, from delivery services and mobile repairs to food trucks and event rentals.

Gearing Up for the Ride: Choosing the perfect vehicle, securing funding, navigating insurance and permits, and equipping your fleet for success.

Charting Your Course: Building a rock-solid business plan, setting competitive rates, creating irresistible packages, and marketing your services to the right audience.

Fueling Your Growth: Hiring and managing employees, expanding your fleet, finding new clients, and implementing strategies to keep your business on the fast track.

Avoiding Roadblocks: Managing risk, navigating legal hurdles, staying organized, and adapting to the ever-changing landscape of the business world.

In this book you would also find useful tools and resources which will offer invaluable insights and guidance for your own journey. So, buckle up, flip the page, and let's hit the road together. This book will be your trusted navigator, helping you navigate the twists and turns of starting a van and truck business. With its practical advice and a healthy dose of inspiration, you'll be cruising towards success in no time.

Remember, the highway of entrepreneurship is full of possibilities, and the wheel is in your hands. Let's go!

Part 1: Understanding The Van And Truck Business

What are Vans and Box Trucks?

Vans and box trucks are types of commercial vehicles commonly used for transportation and logistics purposes.

Vans:

Vans are typically smaller, enclosed vehicles designed for transporting goods, equipment, or people. They come in various sizes, from compact vans suitable for city deliveries to larger models with extended cargo space. Vans are versatile and commonly used by businesses for local deliveries, courier services, tradesmen, and passenger transportation. They offer benefits such as maneuverability, easy loading and unloading, and accessibility to urban areas with restricted access.

Box Trucks:

Box trucks, also known as cube trucks, are larger vehicles with a cargo area enclosed by a rectangular or square-shaped box mounted on the chassis. These trucks vary in size, with capacities ranging from light-duty to heavy-duty, and they often feature a rear roll-up door for loading and unloading cargo. Box trucks provide more significant cargo space compared to vans, making them suitable for transporting large quantities of goods over longer distances. They are commonly used for moving services, freight transportation, retail distribution, and commercial deliveries requiring protection from weather and theft.

Van and box truck business

A vans and box truck business involves operating a fleet of commercial vehicles, including vans and box trucks, to provide transportation, delivery, and logistics services to businesses and individuals. These businesses may offer a range of services, from local delivery and courier services to long-haul transportation and freight logistics.

Key Components of a Vans and Box Truck Business:

- **Fleet Management:** Managing a fleet of vans and box trucks involves acquiring, maintaining, and operating the vehicles efficiently. This includes vehicle procurement, maintenance scheduling, fuel management, and fleet tracking.

- **Driver Management:** Hiring and managing drivers is crucial for ensuring the smooth operation of the business. Driver recruitment, training, scheduling, and performance monitoring are essential aspects of driver management.

- **Route Planning and Optimization:** Optimizing delivery routes to maximize efficiency and minimize costs is essential for vans and box truck businesses. Utilizing route planning software and real-time tracking systems helps optimize routes, reduce fuel consumption, and improve delivery times.

- **Customer Service:** Providing excellent customer service is vital for retaining clients and building a positive reputation in the industry. This involves timely deliveries, accurate order fulfillment, and responsive communication with customers.

- **Logistics Services:** Some vans and box truck businesses offer additional logistics services, such as warehousing, inventory management, and supply chain solutions. These services help clients streamline their operations and improve overall efficiency.

- **Technology Integration:** Integrating technology into operations can enhance efficiency and provide valuable insights into fleet performance. This includes using GPS tracking, telematics systems, fleet management software, and electronic logging devices (ELDs).

- **Compliance and Safety:** Ensuring compliance with regulatory requirements and safety standards is essential for vans and box truck businesses. This includes obtaining necessary permits and licenses, adhering to transportation regulations, and implementing safety protocols for drivers and vehicles.

- **Marketing and Business Development:** Marketing efforts play a crucial role in attracting new clients and expanding the business. This may involve digital marketing, networking, partnerships with other businesses, and participation in industry events and trade shows.

- **Financial Management:** Managing finances effectively is essential for the success of a vans and box truck business. This includes budgeting, accounting, billing, invoicing, and monitoring financial performance to ensure profitability and sustainability.

Market Potential and Benefits

Vans and box trucks offer a multitude of benefits to businesses and individuals involved in transportation, delivery, and logistics operations.
Here are the key advantages of each type of vehicle:
Vans:
Vans provide versatility and flexibility, making them ideal for a wide range of applications. Their compact size and maneuverability allow them to navigate through urban environments and congested streets with ease, making them suitable for last-mile deliveries and urban logistics. Vans can access locations that larger trucks may struggle to reach, enabling efficient door-to-door delivery services for businesses and courier companies.

Another benefit of vans is their accessibility and ease of loading and unloading. Many vans feature sliding side doors and rear doors that can be opened wide, allowing for quick and convenient loading and unloading of cargo. This accessibility is especially advantageous for businesses that require frequent deliveries or need to transport bulky or oversized items.

Vans also offer cost-effectiveness and fuel efficiency compared to larger trucks. They typically have lower operating costs, including fuel consumption, maintenance, and insurance, making them a budget-friendly option for small businesses and independent contractors. Additionally, vans often have better fuel efficiency ratings than larger commercial vehicles, helping businesses save on fuel expenses over time.

Furthermore, vans can be customized and outfitted with various accessories and shelving systems to optimize cargo space and organization. This customization allows businesses to tailor their vans to meet specific operational needs, such as transporting perishable goods, fragile items, or specialized equipment. With the right modifications, vans can serve as mobile workshops, service vehicles, or mobile retail units, providing businesses with added versatility and functionality.

In summary, the benefits of vans include versatility, accessibility, cost-effectiveness, fuel efficiency, and customization options, making them a practical choice for businesses engaged in delivery, transportation, and service-oriented industries.

Box Trucks:

Box trucks offer several advantages that make them indispensable for businesses involved in transporting large volumes of goods over longer distances. One of the primary benefits of box trucks is their spacious cargo capacity and enclosed design, which provides ample space for carrying a wide range of cargo securely. The rectangular or square-shaped cargo area allows for efficient stacking and organization of goods, minimizing the risk of damage during transit.

Another advantage of box trucks is their weatherproof and secure cargo compartment, which protects goods from the elements and unauthorized access. The enclosed design of box trucks makes them suitable for transporting valuable or sensitive items that require protection from moisture, dust, theft, and tampering. This makes box trucks an ideal choice for retail distribution, moving services, and freight transportation.

Box trucks are also known for their versatility and adaptability to various types of cargo and industries. They come in a range of sizes and configurations, from light-duty to heavy-duty models, allowing businesses to choose the right truck for their specific needs. Additionally, box trucks can be equipped with features such as lift gates, refrigeration units, and hydraulic ramps to accommodate different types of cargo and loading/unloading requirements.

Furthermore, box trucks offer reliability and durability, with robust construction and chassis designs that withstand the rigors of commercial use. Their sturdy build and long service life make them a dependable choice for businesses seeking a reliable transportation solution for their goods.

Challenges Of A Van And Box Truck Business.

Operating a van and truck business comes with its share of challenges, which can impact various aspects of the operation. Here are some common challenges faced by businesses in this industry:

Fuel Costs: Fuel prices can fluctuate significantly, affecting operating expenses for vans and trucks. High fuel costs can eat into profit margins, especially for businesses with large fleets or long-distance operations.

Vehicle Maintenance: Maintaining a fleet of vans and trucks requires regular servicing, repairs, and upkeep to ensure optimal performance and safety. Vehicle breakdowns and unexpected repairs can lead to downtime and increased operational costs.

Driver Shortages: Finding and retaining qualified drivers is a persistent challenge in the transportation industry. Driver shortages can lead to difficulties in fulfilling orders, delayed deliveries, and increased labor costs due to higher wages or recruitment efforts.

Regulatory Compliance: Vans and trucks must comply with various regulations and standards, including licensing, permits, weight limits, hours of service regulations, and environmental regulations. Staying compliant with these requirements can be complex and time-consuming.

Safety Concerns: Safety is paramount in the transportation industry, but accidents and incidents can still occur. Ensuring driver safety, implementing safety protocols, and managing risks are ongoing challenges for van and truck businesses.

Competition: The transportation and logistics industry is highly competitive, with numerous companies vying for market share. Competing on price, service quality, and reliability can be challenging, especially for smaller businesses.

Rising Insurance Costs: Insurance costs for commercial vehicles can be substantial, and premiums may increase due to factors such as claims history, vehicle value, and industry trends. Rising insurance costs can impact profitability for van and truck businesses.

Technology Integration: Keeping up with advancements in technology, such as GPS tracking, telematics, and fleet management software, can be challenging for some businesses. Implementing and integrating new technologies effectively requires investment, training, and adaptation.

Environmental Impact: The environmental impact of transportation, including emissions and fuel consumption, is a growing concern. Meeting environmental regulations and adopting sustainable practices, such as investing in alternative fuel vehicles or improving fuel efficiency, presents challenges for van and truck businesses.

Supply Chain Disruptions: External factors such as natural disasters, geopolitical events, or supply chain disruptions can affect the availability of goods, transportation routes, and delivery schedules. Adapting to unforeseen challenges and maintaining operational resilience is crucial for van and truck businesses.

Despite these challenges, van and truck businesses can overcome obstacles by implementing strategic planning, adopting innovative solutions, and staying adaptable in a dynamic industry landscape.

Part 2: The Foundation

Finding Your Niche: Identifying your target market.

In the competitive landscape of the transportation industry, finding your niche is crucial for success in the van and truck business. By identifying a specific market segment or service offering that meets the needs of your target customers, you can differentiate your business, attract loyal clients, and achieve sustainable growth. Finding your niche in the van and truck business requires a combination of market insight, strategic planning, and customer-focused approach.qqThis comprehensive part will outline strategies for finding your niche in the van and truck business and positioning your company for success.

Understanding Your Market

Market Analysis: Conduct thorough market research to identify potential opportunities and challenges in the transportation industry. Analyze market trends, customer preferences, and competitor offerings to gain insights into the competitive landscape.

Identifying Target Customers: Define your target market based on demographics, geographic location, and industry sectors. Consider targeting specific businesses or industries that require transportation services tailored to their unique needs.

Customer Needs Assessment: Understand the pain points and challenges faced by your target customers. Conduct surveys, interviews, or focus groups to gather feedback and identify areas where your business can add value.

Defining Your Service Offerings:

Specialized Transportation Services: Consider offering specialized transportation services tailored to specific industries or types of cargo.

This could include refrigerated transportation for perishable goods, flatbed transportation for oversized items, or hazardous materials transportation for industries such as chemicals or pharmaceuticals.

Last-Mile Delivery Solutions: Explore opportunities in last-mile delivery services for e-commerce companies, retailers, and wholesalers. Offer fast, reliable delivery options to customers' homes or businesses, leveraging technology to optimize route planning and tracking.

Freight Transportation: Position your business as a reliable freight transportation provider for businesses that require the shipment of goods or materials over longer distances. Emphasize efficiency, reliability, and competitive pricing to attract clients in need of freight services.

Moving and Relocation Services: Consider offering moving and relocation services for residential and commercial customers. Provide comprehensive solutions for packing, loading, transporting, and unloading belongings or equipment, catering to customers' unique needs and preferences.

Understanding the Competitive Landscape:

Competitor Analysis: Research existing transportation companies in your area to understand their strengths, weaknesses, and market positioning. Identify gaps in the market or areas where you can differentiate your services to gain a competitive advantage.

Industry Trends: Stay informed about industry trends and emerging technologies that may impact the van and truck business. Keep abreast of advancements in autonomous vehicles, electric vehicles, telematics, and logistics software to remain competitive in a rapidly evolving industry.

Customer Feedback: Pay attention to customer feedback and reviews to understand what clients value most in transportation services. Use this feedback to continually improve your offerings and differentiate your business based on customer satisfaction and service quality.

Positioning Your Business for Success:

Brand Differentiation: Develop a strong brand identity that communicates your unique value proposition and resonates with your target audience. Emphasize your strengths, such as reliability, flexibility, or specialization, to differentiate your business from competitors.

Marketing and Promotion: Implement targeted marketing strategies to reach your ideal customers and showcase your expertise in the van and truck business. Utilize online channels, such as social media, digital advertising, and industry directories, to raise awareness and generate leads.

Customer Relationships: Build strong relationships with your customers based on trust, reliability, and exceptional service. Focus on delivering personalized experiences and exceeding customer expectations to foster long-term loyalty and repeat business.

Continuous Improvement: Stay agile and adaptable in response to changing market conditions, customer needs, and industry trends. Continuously seek opportunities for innovation, efficiency gains, and service enhancements to stay ahead of the competition and position your business for long-term success.

Business Basics: Creating a business plan, legal structure, and financial projections.

Having a business plan before starting a business is essential as it provides a roadmap for success, clarifies the business concept, attracts investors and funding, mitigates risks, sets goals and milestones, and facilitates decision-making. It serves as a strategic tool that outlines your goals, strategies, and action steps, helping you stay focused, organized, and prepared for the challenges ahead. A well-written business plan demonstrates the viability of your business idea, increases the likelihood of attracting external funding, and enables you to make informed decisions about your business's direction and growth.

Creating a Business Plan:

Executive Summary: A concise overview of your business plan, highlighting key elements such as your mission, target market, and objectives.

Company Description: Detailed information about your van and box truck business, including the services you'll offer, your target market, and what sets your business apart from competitors.

Market Analysis: In-depth research into the transportation industry, including market trends, competition, and potential opportunities and threats.

Services Offered: A breakdown of the transportation services your business will provide, tailored to meet the needs of your target market.

Marketing and Sales Strategy: A plan outlining how you'll attract customers and generate revenue, including marketing tactics and sales approaches.

Operational Plan: Details on how your business will operate day-to-day, covering aspects such as fleet management, driver recruitment, and customer service protocols.

Financial Plan: Financial projections for your van and box truck business, including startup costs, revenue forecasts, expenses, and profit and loss projections.

Legal Structure

The importance of a legal structure for a business cannot be overstated as it provides important protections, defines ownership and management roles, and establishes the framework for taxation and regulatory compliance. Selecting the right legal structure, whether it's a sole proprietorship, partnership, limited liability company (LLC), or corporation, is vital for safeguarding personal assets, limiting liability, and minimizing tax liabilities.

Additionally, a clear legal structure helps clarify ownership and management responsibilities, reducing conflicts and ensuring smooth operations. By establishing a solid legal foundation, businesses can mitigate risks, foster transparency, and position themselves for long-term success and growth in a competitive marketplace.

Sole Proprietorship: A business owned and operated by a single individual, offering simplicity but with personal liability for debts and obligations.

Limited Liability Company (LLC): A business structure offering liability protection for owners while allowing flexibility in management and taxation.

Partnership: A business owned by two or more individuals who share profits, losses, and liabilities.

Corporation: A separate legal entity from its owners, providing the most liability protection but with more complex legal and tax requirements.

Choose the legal structure that aligns best with your business goals, risk tolerance, and tax considerations.

Financial Projections:

Financial projections are a useful component of any business plan, providing a roadmap for financial success and guiding decision-making processes. These projections include forecasts for revenue, expenses, cash flow, and profitability, offering insights into the financial health and viability of the business.

By estimating future sales revenue based on market demand and pricing strategies, identifying all startup and operating expenses, projecting cash inflows and outflows to ensure adequate working capital, and determining the level of sales needed to cover expenses and start generating a profit, financial projections help entrepreneurs plan for the future, secure funding, and make informed strategic decisions.

They serve as a benchmark for tracking performance, evaluating business opportunities, and adjusting strategies as needed to achieve financial goals and objectives.

Sales Forecast: Estimates of future sales revenue based on market demand, pricing strategy, and projected sales volume.

Expense Budget: Identification of all startup and operating expenses, including vehicle costs, fuel, insurance, and salaries.

Cash Flow Statement: Projections of cash inflows and outflows on a monthly basis to ensure adequate working capital.

Profit and Loss Projection: Estimates of net profit or loss by subtracting total expenses from total revenue.

Break-Even Analysis: Determination of the level of sales needed to cover expenses and start generating a profit.

.

Securing Funding: Exploring financing options, loans, grants, and bootstrapping strategies.

Starting or expanding a van and truck business often requires significant capital investment. Choosing the right financing option is unavoidable for ensuring the success and growth of your business. Here's a comprehensive guide to help you navigate the various financing options available:

1. Self-Financing:

Using personal savings, investments, or assets to fund your van and truck business is a common option for entrepreneurs. Self-financing offers complete control over your business and avoids the need to pay interest or give up equity. However, it may limit your financial resources and increase personal risk.

2. Business Loans:

Traditional bank loans are a popular financing option for van and truck businesses. Banks offer term loans, lines of credit, and Small Business Administration (SBA) loans to help entrepreneurs cover startup costs, purchase vehicles, or expand operations. Business loans typically require a strong credit history, collateral, and a detailed business plan.

3. Equipment Financing:

Equipment financing allows you to purchase vans and trucks without paying the full cost upfront. Lenders provide loans or leases specifically for acquiring vehicles, with the vehicles themselves serving as collateral. Equipment financing may offer lower interest rates and longer repayment terms than traditional business loans.

4. Invoice Financing:

Invoice financing, or accounts receivable financing, enables you to access funds by selling your unpaid invoices to a third-party lender at a discount. This option can provide immediate cash flow to cover expenses while waiting for customer payments. Invoice financing is particularly useful for van and truck businesses with long payment cycles.

5. Asset-Based Lending:
Asset-based lending involves using your business assets, such as vehicles or accounts receivable, as collateral for a loan. Lenders evaluate the value of your assets to determine the loan amount and terms. Asset-based lending can provide flexibility and liquidity for van and truck businesses with valuable assets but limited cash flow.

6. Peer-to-Peer Lending:
Peer-to-peer (P2P) lending platforms connect borrowers directly with individual investors willing to lend money. P2P loans may offer competitive interest rates and flexible terms, making them an attractive alternative to traditional bank loans. However, P2P lending may have higher interest rates and fees than other financing options.

7. Angel Investors and Venture Capitalists:
Angel investors and venture capitalists are individuals or firms that provide capital to startups and early-stage businesses in exchange for equity ownership. These investors can offer significant funding and expertise to help grow your van and truck business. However, securing investment from angel investors or venture capitalists typically requires a compelling business idea, strong growth potential, and a solid business plan.

8. Government Grants and Programs:
Government grants and programs may provide financial assistance to small businesses in certain industries or geographic areas. Research federal, state, and local government initiatives that support transportation businesses, such as grants for clean energy vehicles or economic development incentives.

Part 3: Building Your Fleet

Choosing the Right Van or Box Truck.

Choosing the right vehicles for your van and box truck business is crucial for ensuring efficient operations, meeting customer needs, and maximizing profitability. Here are key considerations to help you make informed decisions when selecting vehicles:

1. Determine Your Business Needs:
- Assess your business requirements, including the types of goods or materials you'll be transporting, the frequency of deliveries, and the distances traveled.
- Consider factors such as payload capacity, interior dimensions, and fuel efficiency based on your specific transportation needs.

2. Evaluate Vehicle Options:
- Research different types of vehicles available for your van and box truck business, including vans, box trucks, flatbed trucks, and specialized vehicles such as refrigerated trucks or cargo vans with custom shelving.
- Compare features, specifications, and pricing to find vehicles that align with your business needs and budget.

3. Consider Size and Capacity:
- Choose vehicles with sufficient size and capacity to accommodate your cargo while maximizing efficiency and minimizing wasted space.
- Determine the optimal payload capacity and cubic feet of storage space required for your typical loads to ensure you can meet customer demands effectively.

4. Assess Maneuverability and Accessibility:

- Consider the maneuverability of vehicles, especially if you'll be making deliveries in urban or congested areas with tight spaces and narrow streets.
- Evaluate accessibility features such as rear or side doors, ramps, lift gates, and loading docks to facilitate efficient loading and unloading of cargo.

5. Prioritize Safety and Reliability:

- Prioritize safety features such as airbags, anti-lock brakes, stability control, and advanced driver assistance systems (ADAS) to ensure the safety of your drivers and cargo.
- Choose vehicles with a reputation for reliability and durability to minimize downtime and maintenance costs, maximizing productivity and profitability.

6. Consider Environmental Impact:

- Consider the environmental impact of your vehicle choices, including fuel efficiency, emissions, and alternative fuel options such as electric or hybrid vehicles.
- Evaluate the long-term benefits of investing in environmentally friendly vehicles, including potential cost savings, regulatory compliance, and positive brand reputation.

7. Factor in Total Cost of Ownership:

- Evaluate the total cost of ownership, including upfront purchase or lease costs, fuel expenses, insurance premiums, maintenance and repair costs, and resale value.
- Calculate the lifecycle cost of each vehicle option to determine the most cost-effective choice over the long term.

8. Test Drive and Get Feedback:

- Take the time to test drive different vehicle models to experience their performance, comfort, and handling firsthand.

- Seek feedback from drivers, mechanics, and other industry professionals to gain insights into the practical aspects of operating and maintaining each vehicle option.

By carefully considering these factors and conducting thorough research, you can choose the right vehicles for your van and box truck business that align with your business needs, budget, and long-term goals.

Vehicle Acquisition: Buying new or used, lease or purchase.

Vehicle acquisition is a significant decision for any van and box truck business, and several factors must be considered when deciding between buying new or used vehicles and choosing between leasing and purchasing.

Buying New vs. Used Vehicles:

Pros of Buying New:

- **Warranty Coverage:** New vehicles typically come with manufacturer warranties, providing peace of mind and protection against unexpected repairs.
- **Latest Features:** New vehicles often feature the latest technology, safety features, and fuel efficiency improvements, enhancing performance and driver satisfaction.
- **Customization Options:** Buying new allows you to customize vehicles according to your specific requirements, such as adding specialized equipment or accessories.

Cons of Buying New:
- **Higher Initial Cost:** New vehicles come with a higher upfront purchase price compared to used vehicles, increasing your initial investment and potential financing costs.

- **Depreciation:** New vehicles depreciate rapidly in value during the first few years of ownership, resulting in potential losses if you decide to sell or trade them in the future.

Pros of Buying Used:

- **Lower Initial Cost:** Used vehicles are typically more affordable than new vehicles, offering cost savings upfront and potentially lower monthly payments if financed.
- **Reduced Depreciation:** Used vehicles have already experienced significant depreciation, resulting in slower depreciation rates and potentially preserving more of their value over time.
- **More Options:** Buying used provides access to a wider range of makes, models, and configurations, allowing you to find vehicles that meet your needs at a lower price point.

Cons of Buying Used:
- **Limited Warranty Coverage:** Used vehicles may have limited or no warranty coverage, increasing the risk of unexpected repairs and maintenance costs.
- **Potential Issues:** Used vehicles may have a history of wear and tear, previous accidents, or mechanical issues that could require repairs or maintenance shortly after purchase.
- **Financing Challenges:** Financing options for used vehicles may be more limited or come with higher interest rates compared to new vehicles, affecting affordability and overall costs.

Lease vs. Purchase:

Leasing
Leasing typically requires lower upfront costs and lower monthly payments compared to purchasing, making it more affordable for businesses with limited. Lease payments may be tax-deductible as a business expense, providing potential tax benefits and reducing overall tax liabilities. It allows you to upgrade to newer vehicles more frequently, ensuring access to the

latest features and technology without the hassle of selling or trading in vehicles.

Purchase

Purchasing vehicles outright provides ownership and full control over assets, allowing you to customize vehicles, modify them as needed, and potentially retain more value over time. While purchasing may involve higher initial costs, it often results in lower total costs over the long term compared to leasing, especially if vehicles are used for an extended period. Purchased vehicles have no mileage restrictions or usage limits, providing flexibility for businesses with high mileage requirements or unpredictable usage patterns.

Insurance and Permits: Essential coverage for your vehicles and securing operating permits.

In the van and box truck business, ensuring the safety of your vehicles and compliance with regulatory requirements is paramount to success. This comprehensive guide explores the essential coverage needed for your vehicles, including commercial auto insurance, workers' compensation insurance, general liability insurance, and cargo insurance. Additionally, it delves into the permits and authorities required to operate legally, such as DOT numbers, motor carrier authority, state and local permits, and international registration and fuel tax agreements. By understanding and obtaining the necessary insurance and permits, you can protect your assets, mitigate risks, and operate your van and box truck business safely and legally in the transportation industry.

Vehicle Insurance:

Commercial Auto Insurance:
- Commercial auto insurance provides coverage for vehicles used for business purposes, including vans and box trucks.
- Key coverage options include liability coverage for bodily injury and property damage, collision coverage for vehicle damage,

comprehensive coverage for non-collision incidents (e.g., theft, vandalism), and uninsured/underinsured motorist coverage.

- Additional coverage options may include medical payments coverage, roadside assistance, rental reimbursement, and cargo insurance for goods being transported.

Workers' Compensation Insurance:

- Workers' compensation insurance is required in most states and provides coverage for employees who are injured or become ill while performing job-related duties.
- This coverage helps pay for medical expenses, lost wages, disability benefits, and rehabilitation services for injured workers.

General Liability Insurance:

- General liability insurance protects your business against claims of bodily injury, property damage, and personal injury arising from your business operations.
- This coverage extends beyond vehicle-related incidents to cover accidents that occur on your business premises or as a result of your business activities.

Cargo Insurance:

- Cargo insurance provides coverage for goods or merchandise being transported in your vehicles.
- This coverage protects against loss or damage to cargo caused by accidents, theft, fire, or other covered perils.

Operating Permits:

DOT Number:

- A Department of Transportation (DOT) number is required for commercial vehicles weighing over 10,000 pounds or transporting hazardous materials.
- This number is used to track safety compliance and monitor vehicle inspections, maintenance records, and driver qualifications.

Motor Carrier Authority (MC Number):
- Motor carrier authority, also known as an MC number, is required for interstate carriers engaged in transporting passengers or property for hire.
- This authority is issued by the Federal Motor Carrier Safety Administration (FMCSA) and is necessary for operating legally across state lines.

State and Local Permits:
- Depending on your location and the nature of your business, you may need additional permits or licenses from state or local authorities.
- These permits may include business licenses, zoning permits, overweight/oversize permits, or special permits for transporting hazardous materials.

International Registration Plan (IRP) and International Fuel Tax Agreement (IFTA):
- If you operate commercial vehicles across multiple states or provinces, you may need to register your vehicles under the International Registration Plan (IRP) and report fuel taxes under the International Fuel Tax Agreement (IFTA).
- These agreements streamline registration and fuel tax reporting for interstate carriers, ensuring compliance with jurisdictional requirements.

Conclusion:
Insurance and permits are essential for protecting your vehicles, drivers, and business operations while ensuring compliance with legal requirements. By securing comprehensive insurance coverage and obtaining the necessary permits and authorities, you can operate your van and box truck business safely, legally, and efficiently in the transportation industry. Consult with insurance agents, regulatory agencies, and legal advisors to ensure you have the appropriate coverage and permits for your specific business needs and operating environment.

Essential tools, accessories, and technology for efficient operations.

Efficient operations in a van and truck business require the right tools, accessories, and technology to optimize productivity, enhance safety, and meet customer demands. Here are some essential items to consider:

1. GPS Navigation Systems:
GPS navigation systems help drivers plan routes, avoid traffic congestion, and optimize delivery schedules. They provide real-time updates on traffic conditions, road closures, and alternative routes, ensuring timely and efficient deliveries.

2. Fleet Management Software:
Fleet management software allows you to track vehicle location, monitor fuel consumption, schedule maintenance, and analyze driver performance. It provides valuable insights into fleet operations, helping you optimize routes, reduce fuel costs, and improve overall efficiency.

3. Mobile Communication Devices:
Mobile communication devices such as smartphones or two-way radios enable seamless communication between drivers, dispatchers, and customers. They facilitate real-time updates, emergency notifications, and quick responses to changing conditions, enhancing coordination and customer service.

4. Vehicle Tracking Systems:
Vehicle tracking systems use GPS technology to monitor vehicle movements, speed, and fuel usage. They provide valuable data on driver behavior, route efficiency, and vehicle maintenance needs, helping you identify areas for improvement and optimize fleet performance.

5. Cargo Management Accessories:

Cargo management accessories such as shelving, racks, and tie-downs help organize and secure cargo inside vans and trucks. They maximize storage space, minimize shifting during transit, and ensure the safe transport of goods, improving efficiency and customer satisfaction.

6. Safety Equipment:

Safety equipment such as first aid kits, fire extinguishers, reflective vests, and emergency flares are essential for ensuring driver safety and compliance with regulatory requirements. They provide peace of mind and preparedness for unexpected emergencies or accidents on the road.

7. Vehicle Maintenance Tools:

Vehicle maintenance tools such as tire pressure gauges, wrenches, and jumper cables are essential for performing routine maintenance and minor repairs on vans and trucks. They help prevent breakdowns, minimize downtime, and prolong the lifespan of vehicles, reducing operating costs and improving reliability.

8. Telematics Systems:

Telematics systems combine GPS technology with onboard diagnostics to monitor vehicle performance, detect mechanical issues, and provide predictive maintenance alerts. They enable proactive maintenance scheduling, reducing the risk of costly repairs and unplanned downtime.

9. Electronic Logging Devices (ELDs):

Electronic logging devices (ELDs) automate and streamline driver hours-of-service tracking and compliance with government regulations. They record driving hours, rest breaks, and duty status electronically, ensuring compliance with hours-of-service rules and improving driver safety.

10. Fuel Management Systems:

Fuel management systems monitor fuel consumption, track fuel purchases, and detect fuel theft or unauthorized use. They help identify fuel inefficiencies, reduce fuel costs, and prevent fraud, contributing to overall cost savings and operational efficiency.

By equipping your van and truck business with these essential tools, accessories, and technology, you can streamline operations, improve productivity, and maintain a competitive edge in the transportation industry.

Part 4: Launching and Growth

Marketing and Branding: Building brand awareness, attracting customers, and creating a competitive edge.

Marketing and branding are paramount for a van and truck business, serving as the driving force behind success in a competitive industry. Effective marketing strategies help build brand awareness, attract customers, and create a distinct identity in the market. Crafting a compelling brand story, establishing a strong brand presence across various channels, and differentiating from competitors through unique selling propositions, businesses can foster trust, loyalty, and recognition among customers.

Building Brand Awareness

Building brand awareness is the foundation of successful marketing efforts. To achieve this, businesses need to develop a strong brand identity that resonates with their target audience. This involves crafting a compelling brand story, defining brand values and personality, and creating visually appealing brand assets such as logos, colors, and typography.

Consistent branding across all touchpoints, including vehicles, uniforms, website, and marketing materials, helps reinforce brand recognition and familiarity among potential customers. Utilizing various marketing channels such as social media, online advertising, print media, and networking events can further amplify brand exposure and reach a wider audience.

Attracting Customers

Once brand awareness is established, the focus shifts to attracting customers and converting leads into sales. Effective customer acquisition strategies involve understanding the needs and preferences of your target market and tailoring marketing messages and offerings to address their pain points and desires.

Utilizing targeted advertising campaigns, offering promotions or discounts, and leveraging customer testimonials or reviews can entice potential customers to engage with your business. Providing exceptional customer service and delivering on promises are also crucial in building trust and loyalty, turning satisfied customers into brand advocates who refer others to your business.

Creating a Competitive Edge

In a crowded market, creating a competitive edge is essential for differentiation and long-term success. This requires identifying and capitalizing on unique selling propositions (USPs) that set your van and truck business apart from competitors. Whether it's offering faster delivery times, superior customer service, innovative technology solutions, or environmentally friendly practices, highlighting your strengths and value propositions helps position your business as the preferred choice among customers.

Additionally, staying ahead of industry trends, embracing technology advancements, and continuously innovating and improving your offerings demonstrate your commitment to excellence and keep you ahead of the competition.

Setting Rates and Packages.

Setting rates and packages for a van and truck business requires careful consideration of cost analysis, competitive pricing strategies, and tailored quoting for different jobs.

1. Cost Analysis

Before setting rates and packages, it's essential to conduct a thorough cost analysis to understand the expenses associated with operating your van and truck business. This includes fixed costs such as vehicle maintenance, insurance, permits, and overhead expenses, as well as variable costs such as fuel, labor, and materials. By calculating the total cost per mile or per hour of operation, you can establish a baseline for pricing that ensures profitability while covering all expenses and overhead.

2. Competitive Pricing Strategies:

Competitive pricing strategies involve analyzing the pricing landscape within the transportation industry and positioning your rates relative to competitors. This may involve pricing your services slightly below, at, or above market rates depending on factors such as your level of expertise, service quality, and unique value propositions. Additionally, consider the perceived value of your services compared to competitors and adjust pricing accordingly to attract customers while maintaining profitability.

3. Quoting for Different Jobs:

Quoting for different jobs requires flexibility and customization to accommodate the varying needs and requirements of clients. When preparing quotes, consider factors such as distance traveled, delivery urgency, cargo size and weight, labor intensity, and any additional services requested by the client. Tailor your quotes to provide transparent pricing that reflects the specific details of each job, including any surcharges or additional fees for special requests or circumstances. Providing detailed, accurate, and competitive quotes helps build trust with clients and increases the likelihood of winning contracts.

Finding Customers.

Finding customers for a van and truck business requires a proactive approach that combines direct sales efforts, online marketing strategies, strategic partnerships, and networking initiatives. By diversifying your customer acquisition channels and leveraging various strategies to reach potential customers, you can effectively grow your business and establish a strong presence in the transportation industry. Finding customers for a van and truck business requires a multifaceted approach that encompasses direct sales, leveraging online platforms, building strategic partnerships, and networking effectively. Here's a breakdown of each strategy:

1. Direct Sales:

Direct sales involve proactively reaching out to potential customers through targeted marketing efforts, cold calling, and door-to-door sales. Identify businesses and individuals in your target market who may require transportation services and reach out to them directly to offer your services. Tailor your sales pitch to highlight the unique value proposition of your van and truck business and demonstrate how your services can meet their specific needs and requirements.

2. Online Platforms:

Utilize online platforms such as business directories, industry-specific websites, and social media channels to expand your reach and attract customers. Create a professional website for your van and truck business that showcases your services, expertise, and customer testimonials. Optimize your online presence for search engines to increase visibility and attract organic traffic. Additionally, consider leveraging online marketplaces and platforms that connect businesses and individuals in need of transportation services with service providers like yours.

3. Building Partnerships:

Build strategic partnerships with complementary businesses and organizations that can refer customers to your van and truck business. This may include freight brokers, logistics companies, moving companies, construction firms, retailers, and e-commerce businesses. Establish mutually beneficial relationships by offering incentives or discounts for referrals and collaborating on marketing initiatives to reach a wider audience. By leveraging the networks and resources of your partners, you can generate leads and secure new customers more effectively.

4. Networking Strategies:

Networking is a powerful way to connect with potential customers and industry professionals, build relationships, and generate leads for your van and truck business. Attend industry events, trade shows, and networking meetings to meet key decision-makers and influencers in the transportation industry. Join industry associations and online forums to participate in discussions, share insights, and establish your credibility as a trusted service provider. Cultivate relationships with fellow professionals, suppliers, and existing customers to tap into their networks and expand your customer base through word-of-mouth referrals.

Operational Excellence

Operational excellence is paramount for the success of any van and truck business, ensuring efficiency, reliability, and customer satisfaction. It encompasses various elements such as effective dispatching, meticulous tracking, efficient scheduling, prudent fuel management, and comprehensive driver training. By judiciously optimizing these operational aspects, businesses can streamline processes, minimize costs, maximize productivity, and deliver superior service to customers. Operational excellence not only enhances overall performance but also strengthens competitiveness and fosters long-term success in the transportation industry.

Dispatching

Effective dispatching involves assigning and coordinating drivers and vehicles to fulfill customer orders or service requests efficiently. This includes prioritizing tasks based on urgency, proximity, and available resources, as well as optimizing routes to minimize travel time and fuel consumption. Utilizing dispatching software or systems helps streamline operations, automate dispatching tasks, and provide real-time visibility into driver locations and job statuses.

Tracking

Tracking vehicle movements and job progress is crucial for monitoring operations, ensuring accountability, and providing timely updates to customers. GPS tracking systems enable real-time tracking of vehicle locations, routes taken, and delivery statuses, allowing dispatchers to make informed decisions, proactively address issues, and communicate accurate arrival times to customers. Additionally, tracking systems help improve driver safety, deter theft, and optimize fleet efficiency by identifying areas for route optimization and performance improvement.

Scheduling

Efficient scheduling involves planning and organizing driver schedules, job assignments, and maintenance tasks to maximize productivity and minimize downtime. Utilizing scheduling software or tools helps automate scheduling processes, optimize resource allocation, and ensure compliance with regulatory requirements and customer deadlines. By balancing workloads, avoiding overbooking, and prioritizing tasks effectively, businesses can improve operational efficiency, customer satisfaction, and overall profitability.

Fuel Management

Fuel management is critical for controlling operating costs, reducing environmental impact, and optimizing fleet performance. Implementing fuel management systems or practices helps monitor fuel consumption, identify inefficiencies, and implement strategies to minimize fuel waste and unauthorized fuel usage. This may include establishing fuel-efficient driving practices, conducting regular vehicle maintenance, and investing in fuel-saving technologies such as hybrid or electric vehicles. By actively managing fuel usage and costs, businesses can achieve significant cost savings and contribute to sustainability goals.

Driver Training:

Comprehensive driver training programs are essential for promoting safety, compliance, and professionalism among drivers. Training programs cover a range of topics, including defensive driving techniques, vehicle operation and maintenance, customer service skills, and regulatory compliance. By providing ongoing training and development opportunities, businesses can improve driver performance, reduce the risk of accidents and violations, and enhance overall service quality and customer satisfaction.

Part 5: Scaling Up and Sustainability

Scaling up refers to the process of increasing the size, capacity, or scope of a business to accommodate growth and expansion. This may involve expanding operations, increasing production capacity, entering new markets, or diversifying product offerings to meet growing demand and capitalize on opportunities for increased revenue and market share.

Sustainability, on the other hand, refers to the ability of a business to maintain long-term viability and success while minimizing negative impacts on the environment, society, and economy. It involves balancing economic growth with environmental stewardship, social responsibility, and ethical business practices to ensure that resources are used efficiently and responsibly, and that the needs of present and future generations are met.

In essence, scaling up focuses on growth and expansion, while sustainability focuses on ensuring that growth is environmentally and socially responsible, and that the business can continue to thrive in the long term.

Hiring and Managing Employees

Hiring and managing employees for a van and truck business is a critical aspect of ensuring efficient operations, maintaining safety standards, and delivering exceptional service to customers. Here's a comprehensive guide to effectively recruit, onboard, and manage employees in the transportation industry:

Recruiting Drivers:

Recruiting skilled and reliable drivers is essential for ensuring the safe and efficient operation of your van and truck business. Develop a targeted recruitment strategy to attract qualified candidates, including posting job listings on online job boards, attending career fairs, and leveraging social media platforms.

a. Define Job Requirements: Clearly outline the qualifications, experience, and skills required for driver positions, including a valid commercial driver's license (CDL), clean driving record, and relevant experience in the transportation industry.

b. Utilize Multiple Channels: Advertise job openings through various channels such as online job boards, industry-specific websites, social media platforms, and local community resources to attract a diverse pool of candidates.

c. Conduct Thorough Screening: Screen candidates rigorously through interviews, background checks, driving record checks, and drug tests to ensure they meet safety and compliance standards.

d. Highlight Benefits and Advancement Opportunities: Emphasize the competitive wages, benefits, and opportunities for career advancement available to drivers within your company to attract and retain top talent.

Building a Team

Building a cohesive and high-performing team is essential for achieving operational excellence and delivering exceptional service to customers. To build an effective team, you have to take the following into consideration.

Foster a Positive Work Environment: Cultivate a positive work culture that values teamwork, respect, and collaboration among employees. Encourage open communication, transparency, and mutual support to foster a sense of camaraderie and belonging.

Provide Ongoing Training and Development: Invest in continuous training and development programs to enhance employees' skills, knowledge, and job performance. Offer opportunities for professional growth and advancement within the organization to motivate and retain employees.

Promote Work-Life Balance: Prioritize work-life balance by offering flexible scheduling options, paid time off, and supportive policies that accommodate employees' personal and family needs.

Encourage Employee Engagement: Engage employees in decision-making processes, solicit feedback and input on operational improvements, and recognize and reward their contributions and achievements to foster a sense of ownership and commitment to the company's success.

Managing Employee Performance:

a. Set Clear Expectations: Clearly communicate performance expectations, goals, and metrics to employees, and provide regular feedback and performance evaluations to track progress and address areas for improvement.

b. Address Performance Issues Promptly: Address performance issues or conduct violations promptly and constructively through coaching, counseling, or disciplinary action as necessary, while ensuring compliance with employment laws and regulations.

c. Provide Resources and Support: Equip employees with the tools, resources, and support they need to succeed in their roles, including access to training, technology, and assistance with job-related challenges.

d. Recognize and Reward Excellence: Acknowledge and reward employees for their outstanding performance, dedication, and contributions to the success of the company through incentives, bonuses, awards, or other forms of recognition.

Ensuring Safety and Compliance

Safety and compliance of employees are paramount considerations for any business, particularly in industries such as transportation where workers face inherent risks. Compliance, on the other hand, entails adhering to applicable laws, regulations, and industry standards governing workplace safety, hours of service, driver qualifications, and vehicle maintenance.

Ensuring safety involves implementing comprehensive policies, procedures, and training programs to mitigate hazards, prevent accidents, and protect employees from harm. This includes

a. Prioritizing Safety: Prioritize safety as a core value of your organization by implementing comprehensive safety policies, procedures, and training programs to mitigate risks and ensure the well-being of employees and the public.

b. Maintain Compliance: Stay abreast of federal, state, and local regulations governing the transportation industry, including hours-of-service regulations, vehicle maintenance requirements, and driver qualification standards, and ensure compliance through ongoing training, monitoring, and audits.

c. Provide Supportive Resources: Offer resources and support to drivers to help them navigate regulatory requirements, address compliance issues, and maintain their licenses and certifications.

d. Foster a Safety Culture: Foster a culture of safety among employees by promoting awareness, accountability, and proactive measures to prevent accidents, injuries, and violations.

Expanding Your Business

Expanding a van and truck business requires careful planning, strategic decision-making, and effective execution to capitalize on growth opportunities and achieve long-term success.

Begin by conducting thorough market research to identify growth opportunities, assess market demand, and evaluate the competitive landscape. Analyze industry trends, customer needs, and emerging market segments to identify areas for expansion and differentiation.

Based on market research findings, develop a clear and focused growth strategy that outlines your expansion goals, target markets, and key initiatives. Determine whether you will expand geographically, diversify services, target new customer segments, or introduce new product offerings.

Expand your fleet of vans and trucks to meet growing demand and serve new markets effectively. Consider purchasing new vehicles, leasing additional equipment, or partnering with fleet management companies to increase capacity and improve operational efficiency.

As you expand your operations, hire and train additional drivers, dispatchers, and support staff to handle increased workload and ensure smooth operations. Invest in comprehensive training programs to onboard new employees and enhance their skills and knowledge.

Leverage technology solutions such as fleet management software, GPS tracking systems, and route optimization tools to streamline operations, improve efficiency, and optimize resource utilization. Automate administrative tasks, track vehicle performance, and monitor driver behavior to enhance productivity and customer service.

Forge strategic partnerships with complementary businesses, suppliers, and industry stakeholders to expand your network, access new markets, and create synergies. Collaborate with freight brokers, logistics providers, and e-commerce platforms to tap into new revenue streams and enhance service offerings.

Focus on delivering exceptional customer service to retain existing customers and attract new business. Develop personalized solutions, offer flexible scheduling options, and provide value-added services to differentiate your business and build customer loyalty.

Stay informed about regulatory requirements and industry standards governing the transportation sector, including safety regulations, licensing requirements, and environmental regulations. Ensure compliance with all applicable laws and regulations to avoid penalties and maintain credibility.

Regularly monitor key performance indicators (KPIs) such as revenue growth, customer satisfaction, and fleet utilization to track progress towards expansion goals. Evaluate the effectiveness of your growth strategies, identify areas for improvement, and make necessary adjustments to optimize performance and drive continued growth.

Encourage innovation and continuous improvement within your organization to adapt to changing market dynamics, technological advancements, and customer preferences. Empower employees to contribute ideas, experiment with new approaches, and embrace change to stay ahead of the competition.

Financial Management and Taxes

Financial management and taxes are critical aspects of running a successful van and truck business. By effectively managing finances and navigating tax obligations, van and truck businesses can maintain financial stability, optimize profitability, and achieve long-term success in the transportation industry. Here's a detailed overview of how to effectively manage finances and navigate tax obligations:

1. Budgeting and Cash Flow Management:

Develop a comprehensive budget that outlines all revenue streams, expenses, and financial obligations associated with operating your van and truck business. Monitor cash flow regularly to ensure sufficient liquidity for day-to-day operations, vehicle maintenance, and unforeseen expenses. Implement cash flow management strategies such as invoicing promptly, negotiating favorable payment terms with suppliers, and maintaining adequate reserves to manage fluctuations in income and expenses.

2. Expense Management:

Closely monitor and control expenses to optimize profitability and minimize waste. Identify areas where costs can be reduced or eliminated without compromising quality or safety. Implement cost-saving measures such as fuel efficiency initiatives, vehicle maintenance schedules, and inventory management systems to control operating expenses and improve bottom-line performance.

3. Financial Reporting and Analysis:

Generate regular financial reports, including income statements, balance sheets, and cash flow statements, to track financial performance and identify trends. Conduct financial analysis to assess profitability, efficiency, and liquidity ratios, and benchmark your business against industry standards to identify areas for improvement and strategic decision-making.

4. Tax Planning and Compliance:

Develop a tax planning strategy to minimize tax liabilities and maximize deductions while ensuring compliance with tax laws and regulations. Work with a qualified accountant or tax advisor to identify eligible deductions, credits, and incentives available to van and truck businesses, such as fuel tax credits, depreciation allowances, and small business deductions. Stay informed about changes in tax laws and regulations that may impact your business and proactively adjust your tax strategy accordingly.

5. Recordkeeping and Documentation:

Maintain accurate and organized financial records, including receipts, invoices, bank statements, and tax documents, to support tax filings and financial reporting requirements. Use accounting software or cloud-based systems to streamline recordkeeping processes and ensure data integrity and security. Retain records for the required period as specified by tax authorities and regulatory agencies to facilitate audits and inquiries.

6. Capital Investment and Financing:

Evaluate capital investment opportunities, such as purchasing new vehicles, expanding facilities, or investing in technology upgrades, to support business growth and competitiveness. Consider various financing options, including traditional bank loans, lines of credit, leasing arrangements, and government-sponsored programs, to fund capital expenditures and working capital needs. Compare interest rates, terms, and repayment schedules to select the most suitable financing option for your business.

7. Risk Management and Insurance:

Mitigate financial risks associated with operating a van and truck business by obtaining adequate insurance coverage, including commercial auto insurance, liability insurance, cargo insurance, and workers' compensation insurance. Review insurance policies annually to ensure coverage aligns with business needs and regulatory requirements and consider additional coverage or endorsements to address specific risks or exposures.

Risk Management and Safety.

Risk management and safety are paramount considerations for van and truck businesses to ensure the protection of assets, personnel, and reputation.

Insurance Coverage

Obtain comprehensive insurance coverage tailored to the specific needs of your van and truck business. Key insurance policies to consider include:

- **Commercial Auto Insurance:** Provides coverage for vehicles used in business operations, including liability for bodily injury and property damage, collision coverage, and comprehensive coverage for non-collision incidents such as theft or vandalism.

- **Liability Insurance:** Protects against claims and lawsuits arising from accidents, injuries, or property damage caused by your business operations.

- **Cargo Insurance:** Covers loss or damage to goods or cargo being transported by your vehicles.

- **Workers' Compensation Insurance:** Provides coverage for medical expenses, lost wages, and disability benefits for employees injured on the job.

Regularly review and update insurance policies to ensure adequate coverage levels and compliance with regulatory requirements.

Driver Safety Protocols

Driver safety protocols are essential for ensuring the safety of drivers, passengers, and other road users, as well as protecting the reputation and assets of van and truck businesses. Key components of driver safety protocols are:

Pre-Employment Screening:
Before hiring drivers, conduct thorough pre-employment screenings to assess their qualifications, experience, and driving history. This may include:

- **Background Checks:** Verify employment history, driving record, and criminal background to ensure candidates meet safety and compliance standards.

- **Driving Record Checks:** Review candidates' driving records to assess their history of traffic violations, accidents, and license suspensions or revocations.

- **Drug and Alcohol Testing:** Require candidates to undergo drug and alcohol testing as part of the screening process to ensure they are fit to operate commercial vehicles safely.

Comprehensive Training Programs:

Provide comprehensive training programs to equip drivers with the skills, knowledge, and competencies necessary to operate vehicles safely. Training topics include:

- **Defensive Driving Techniques:** Teach defensive driving techniques to help drivers anticipate and respond to potential hazards, minimize risks, and avoid accidents.

- **Vehicle Operation:** Train drivers on proper vehicle operation, including vehicle controls, handling characteristics, and safe driving practices for different road and weather conditions.

- **Cargo Handling and Securement:** Educate drivers on proper cargo handling procedures, load securement techniques, and weight distribution to prevent shifting, spills, and accidents during transit.

- **Emergency Procedures:** Provide training on emergency procedures, including accident response, vehicle evacuation, first aid, and emergency communication protocols.

Monitoring and Enforcement:
Implement monitoring and enforcement mechanisms to track driver performance, identify risky behaviors, and enforce compliance with safety protocols. This may include:

- **Telematics Systems:** Install telematics systems and onboard technology to monitor driver behavior, vehicle performance, and compliance with safety regulations in real-time.

- **GPS Tracking:** Use GPS tracking devices to monitor driver locations, routes, and adherence to planned schedules, and identify deviations or unauthorized stops.

- **Performance Metrics:** Establish key performance indicators (KPIs) for driver safety, such as accident rates, speeding incidents, and fuel efficiency, and use performance metrics to evaluate and incentivize safe driving behaviors.

Incentive Programs: Offer incentives, bonuses, or rewards to drivers who meet or exceed safety targets, achieve accident-free milestones, or participate in additional safety training and development opportunities.

Continuous Improvement and Feedback:
Encourage a culture of continuous improvement and feedback to solicit input from drivers, identify areas for improvement, and implement corrective actions as necessary. This may include:

- Providing channels for drivers to submit feedback, suggestions, and safety concerns anonymously to management to address issues promptly and proactively.

- Establishing protocols for reporting accidents, near-misses, and safety incidents to investigate root causes, identify trends, and implement corrective actions to prevent future occurrences.

Emergency Preparedness:

Develop and implement emergency preparedness plans to respond effectively to accidents, breakdowns, natural disasters, and other unforeseen events. Key components of emergency preparedness plans include:

Emergency Response Procedures: Establish clear protocols for drivers to follow in the event of an accident, breakdown, or other emergencies. Provide drivers with emergency contact information, roadside assistance resources, and instructions for reporting incidents promptly.

Vehicle Maintenance: Implement a proactive vehicle maintenance program to prevent mechanical failures and ensure vehicles are in safe operating condition. Conduct regular inspections, servicing, and repairs to address issues promptly and minimize the risk of breakdowns or accidents.

Communication and Coordination: Establish communication channels and protocols for coordinating response efforts between drivers, dispatchers, emergency services, and other relevant stakeholders. Ensure all personnel are trained on emergency procedures and know their roles and responsibilities in a crisis situation.

Contingency Planning: Develop contingency plans and backup strategies to address potential disruptions to operations, such as road closures, severe weather, or supply chain interruptions. Maintain contingency supplies, alternative routes, and backup resources to minimize downtime and maintain service continuity.

Bonus Page

Vehicle maintenance
CHECKLIST

DATE: _____

№	DAILY ACTIVITIES (BEFORE THE DAY'S WORK)	✓
1	Walk around the vehicles for inspection	
2	Check for leaks, Flat tires, Loose objects or bolts under the vehicle	
3	Check for damages on the body of the vehicles	
4	Check all lights (headlights, Turn signals, Brake lights etc.)	
5	Windshield wiper's check for wear and Tear	
6	Check washer fluid	
7	Check engine oil	
8	Check Tire pressure (with a guage)